MW01050559

BAD
POEMS ARE
BAD

BLAINE DOLLAR

CONTENTS

BAD POEMS
AND SOME OTHER STUFF

.

This book is available on
Amazon.com,
Barnesandnobles.com,
or the Kindle format.

ISBN: 1505894972
ISBN-13: 978-1505894974

I Am Not a Writer

I am not an author.
I am not a speaker.
I am not singer.
I am not a preacher.
I am not a writer...

I do write.

But I am not a writer.
I do not have elaborate stories;
I do not have the mind for fairy tales;
I do not abide by a form or rhythm.
I cannot write a play.
I just write,
and write;
I write whatever I need to say.

A Poem

I can offer you flowers,
I can shower you with gifts,
I can cook you dinner, lunch, or breakfast.
I can hold you.
I can kiss you.
I can give you everything you want or need.

I can give you part of me.
I can give you something of value;
greater value than anything you crave.

I have saved it for a while;
for a moment that you need to see my love.

It is part of me.
It something you can keep when we're apart.
I can offer you anything...
But, what's worth more than a poem from the heart?

The Boy with the Button Shirt

Whether happy, excited, or hurt,
the simple boy always wore a buttoned-up shirt.
He was very average, nothing really unique.
He was very messy, never neat.
He played at night.
He played during the day.
He played with his kite.
He played in the hay.
Although, no matter where he played,
in the house, with blocks, or in mud and dirt.
He always was just a simple boy, with his buttoned-up shirt.

These Are the Feelings I Feel

I do not have words worthy of comparison
to even the most mediocre of poets.
If I could express it like the artists express it...
maybe I could show it.
If I could write how the writers write...
then maybe I could confess it.
And maybe one day I may possess it,
or maybe upon a 'dreary night,'
possess that power that is required for writers
to write how writers write.
It is sad to say... I cannot reveal that gift,
even though I may feel those feelings, I cannot sift
through words or shift them around to form the perfect depiction
of the bluest skies, the greenest grass, or the flawless loving fiction.

The writers speak with such finesse,
"Let us gaze into the stars and caress
each other under moonlight and stars.
Away from buildings! Away from cars!
Let our love flourish and it shall last forever.
In my heart, I believe in our love, without a doubt."

I may feel those feelings, but I still say,
"Wanna hang out?"

The writer says, "How art thou, beautiful angel?"
The girls go wooing...
But no girl listens to:
"How you doing?"

"Lost are the words to describe the sorrow
and pain that I undergo in this rejection"

"Rejected because I lack the collection
of words to say how I feel."

"Bestowed this treacherous curse of being
a straw in a bundle of hay. The end draws nigh!"

"It sucks being just a normal guy..."

And it is very sad to say that, by God,
I am constricted to just simply cry.
I do not have a beautiful description,
for I am cursed as a normal guy.
A normal guy with normal feelings.
And sadly, these feelings cannot be written
or spoken in any outstanding way.
If I am sad, then I am just sad,
because that is all a normal guy can say.

Should I Stay or Should I Go?

I've reached a point in my life
where everything is black and white;
this or that.

But regardless of my decisions,
right or wrong –
an enormous amount of repercussions come from it.

"Do I tell her I like her?"
"Should I apply for this job?"
"What if I moved *here* or *there*?"

Why can't I ever be just happy?
Why can't the world just be simpler?
This world; this society; does everything to bring you down.
So, we're afraid to ever try to make decisions...
because we're scared.
We're scared what effect this decision, or choice, will have on our
life.
Therefore, we're all stuck in this never ending cycle
of never making choices that may better our lives.
And so, we sit in sadness... because our lives continue to suck.
What is this?

And now, I'm stuck again,
with another choice to make.
"Should I stay or should I go?"
After all this sadness, should I make a change?
I'm fed up with being scared... but...
Should I stay or should I go?

Wait. Never mind... it's Sunday.
Chick-fil-a is closed.

Hello Rose/I am Blue

This Rose is red, and I am blue...
since I can't stand a moment without thinking of you.

On our first meeting, merely a minute had passed...
And there it was... the wait... over... at last...

Your eyes opened.
Bloomed.
I was consumed.
Consumed by the elegant and flowing aroma of your perfume.
Oh that perfume...

No blossomed flower has petals as charmingly as yours.
The way they caress your rosy cheeks.

This Rose is different...
It could never wither or age, nor could it flurry.
But could it wither away? Away from me?
That was my worry...

Another fear that I hold close, is that... could I guarantee
that just like I do to it, does this Rose sway to me?
Could it just be the wind imitating its fixation?
Is this carnation's adoration
simply a figment of my imagination?

Is it simply a flower?

No... This Rose is different...
This Rose... This Rose... is red.
And I am blue...
As I do not know if I ever had you.

Oly Fingerwheel

Now, what I'm about to tell you
may seem a little... surreal.
This is Oly...
A finger... on a wheel.
He may seem creepy,
and somewhat eerie.
Yet, despite his appearance,
he's rather cheery.
He rolls around
and plays in his sand.
Pondering on the thought,
"Am I from the left, or right hand?"
And the questions would continue
as his little wheels would spin,
"And from whose hand
would it have been?"
But as he saw the sun set,
his thoughts decided to swap.
It was time for little Oly to go home,
to his box, with little holes on top.

So he began to roll on home,
leaving in the sand, two continuous streaks,
and after each pull would be
two, delightful, in sync, squeaks.

As he approached his house
and his sign covered in ink.
He stopped and gazed...
He began to think.

"I am just a finger on a wheel.
I live in a box,
I play in sand,
and I don't own any socks!

I have no opinion of
any season.
And in this giant world,
I may have no reason.
I'm ok with that, though.
I'll always be happy, in the hot or cold.
Because why not?"

And inside, little Oly Fingerwheel rolled.

Mommy

Mommy!
Mommy!
Why can't you hear me?

I already know why...
But I thought I would try
to see if you would reply...
to any degree...
Why can't you hear me mommy...?

I miss you...
Daddy keeps yelling...
Daddy keeps swinging...
It keeps on stinging...
Why can't you hear my screaming, mommy?
Am I not desperate enough?
Am I not loud enough, mommy?

I thought you loved me...
You said you did...
and I believed you.
You said you would be right back, mommy...
You said you would...
I still believe you...

How could you let this happen, mommy?
I have no more room for this red water to spill.
I have no more room for bruises, and he'll
keep on hitting me... mommy... will
you come back...
please... for me...

I can't cry anymore...
I can't... because you never came back...
But I got these new brown clothes...
And a new stone hat...
It has my name on it...
It has my name on the stone hat...
carved in black...

Mommy... why did you never come back?

I Want to be an Aardvark

If I was an aardvark,
I would do whatever aardvarks do.
But I'd be the best of the best,
better than all the rest, it's true!
Other people want to be spiders or wolves!
Maybe something that growls,
or hisses, or something that flew.
No one wants to be aardvark.
But I do!
That makes me cool!
At least from my point of view.
Yep… I'd be a cool aardvark.
And do whatever aardvarks do.

Princess Kitty Lives in a Hovel

Princess Kitty lives in a hovel.
It isn't much, but it's her home.
It isn't too awful...
She has bugs, of all sorts, to call her own.

Like... Timmy, the flea,
and Tom, the fly!
However, Princess Kitty has no choice
but to sleep where these bed bugs lie.

They bite and crawl, and leave
little marks from the pain they inflict.
Leaving poor Princess Kitty
looking like a recovering meth addict.

The floors are dirt.
The walls are cracked.
With all these faults,
it's a surprise the house keeps intact.

With all the creaks and squeaks,
it's a problem for Kitty to sleep.
She learns to enjoy it, though...
because the rent is cheap.

Illustration by Katie Dornbierer

Halt

Heart drop.
Beat stop.

You make
the mind swap.

One crime.
One time.

Met eyes.
Vaporized.
Sublime.

It was my fault;
Default.

Self-wound;
add salt.

Now I am

Speechless,
Sleepless,
Weakness.

This pain is ceaseless.

We don't have
to meet eyes.
Just pass by.

Surprise.

Disguise.

You try.
I improvise.
Just lies.

Paralyzed.

Walk away.
Afraid.
I fade
Into shade.
There I stay.

Touch the blade.
Insane.

Dissociate.

Heart drop.
Beat stop.
Meet eyes.
I cry.

We're through.
Your view.
Cut through.

Can't stand
loving you.

Fish

How pleasantly gentle this water feels... conforming to my scales.
My fins... like hands in the wind...
Flowing gracefully to the imaginary hills and swerves...
Little effort it takes to dance, when water leads to the sound of
nature.
I am merely its ribbon.
Dance with me...

To a rest, near the blanket of waves and the rippled, radiant rays...
The heat... only but a light touch on my figure.
Settled eyes...
Released... to the sight of a descending... divine, silhouette.

A worm...
Swaying...
Dance with me...
The sprits grace me with light, to see your heart beating for me.
"Come! Let us dance together..."
We shall dance... we shall be one... you and I, and the waters!

Raise the curtains! One cannot float so elegantly without fins...
This must be a show... an act!
Bravo! Bravo Worm!
How delicious you seem... and how much I crave your body and
heart...

What a show it would have been...
But I see your lure, fisherman.

I see the stripes of orange and white...
I see the string you so thirstily tug.

I will not be baited along by the song of your strummed harp...
I, now, realize how vile the song truly is.
How much I wanted to dance...
But I do not want to dance to this song anymore.

Freely Writing

I read a poem not even moments ago,
about planes, and being "free!"
It rhymed every time!
It even spoke to me!

So, I turned to a page of white
with lines of red and blue.
I motioned to write...
Fuck you!

I wrote nothing!
This can't be...
Fucking planes spoke to me?!

That hit a nerve?
Nothing about reins, chains, or strains...
Fucking planes?!

Hell, a lot of shit is free...
Most animals... most countries...
Hell, food samples at the supermarket are free!
And I can't write a damn thing!
But planes spoke to me...

Food samples won't hit a nerve...
That won't make someone's day.
Hors d'oeuvre's on a tray,
or a mix
of sushi or chicken on toothpicks!
No one would give a shit.

Let me show you...

This is a Title of a Poem

Resting upon a silver platter, given to us at birth,
while wanderer's wonder what we're worth.
We're not held back by our flagless shafts,
and some stranger's conviction will not endanger our paths.
We are free to choose what we contain,
whether chicken, sushi, or sugar cane.
We may withhold any taste.
We may be based with, laced with, or placed with
tangy, candy, crunchy, chunky, spicy,
or nicely with a touch of a pricey topping.
We sit here while you're shopping,
and no one is stopping us from hopping away.
We choose to stay on our platter for you,
it's what we want to do.
We are free, and so are you!
And all of us can choose to be friendly and giving,
otherwise, what's the point of living?

Nevertheless of our meaning,
and our point of breathing,
and whether or not we're nutritious
it's the fact that we're delicious,
and because we're free!
Take a taste of me!

Then maybe I can take a bite out of you,
because you look delicious, too.

History

Tell me your secrets,
Tell me your tale,
Tell me your story,
Tell me where you have failed.

Have you slayed a dragon?
Have you murdered a man?
Tell me how much blood you've shed.
How much blood is on your hand?

Have you traveled the seas?
Have you danced with queens?
Do you withhold treasure
that has never been seen?

Tell me your secrets,
and I'll tell you mine.
Shall I go first then?
That is fine.

Now, no one shall know
this moment I shall reveal.
So once you hear these words
let your mind and mouth forever be sealed.

Long ago, centuries it seems,
I was watching a horror movie
and I shit myself. It was a full theater...
Literally. It was everywhere...
You could smell it...

Dude, it was bad.

White Envy

white...
a white canvas...

WHITE!!
NOTHING ELSE?!

I have no paint...
Why don't I have paint?

Paint me starry...
Paint me as a vase with golden flowers...
Paint me as a lover... of a poor man of ambition.
Paint me black...
Paint me green... or red...
A single stroke...
paint me something

I have no sky...
no mountains or crimson sunset.

and you claim me as art?
I am untitled...
I am plain...
I am not given any nails to be hung...
No moment to be analyzed... or appreciated.

or awed at...

You have the brush in hand!
You are the creator!
The ultimate artist!

You painted them!
Why not me?!

I... I'm not angry...
I'm not sad...
I'm jealous...
I want a meaning...
They have meanings!
They are beautiful! And cherished for it!

I want to be cherished...
Valued by you... fuck... by anyone!

No one loves me... because
       i am plain...
             i am nothing...

...I'm sorry...

I am not angry...
I am not jealous...
I... I Envy them...
I want to be them...
I want to be a piece of art...
abstract... realistic... I don't care...
I just don't want to be me...
I just don't want to be... Envy.

Chad, the Come-eat-ian

Hey there, reader!
Welcome to the show!
What is it about?
No-body, nose!
or maybe about fingers or toes...

I am an artist!
And like a broom,
I will ***sweep*** the nation;
up for nominations,
with endless, standing ovations!

I tell all sorts of jokes!
And I'll never quit!
Although, I won't tell you the one of the cow,
I always ***butcher*** it...

I tell others my jokes;
like Oly, because he understands...
But when I'm with him,
things ***get out of hand***...
I get way too excited
And my jokes seem to go down south...
So I just stick to having my fame
be shared through ***word of mouth***.

Some tell me to get a partner
for my shows, but I think they would slack...
I tried working with a Spine once,
that really ***held me back***.

I know it's extreme
that I don't work in teams...
But I seem to be the only one
who cares about my dreams...

I could have done anything;
but this is what I wanted...
To be a comedian...
I keep pushing, even if daunted...

I also thought of other ideas
and they contained just as much terror...
Whether stand-up, or a **cooking show**,
no matter the dreams... to be successful...
there is little **margarine** for error...

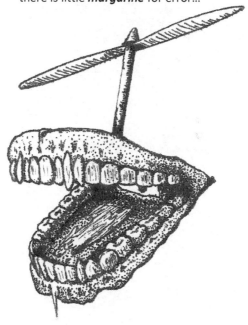

Excerpt from Journal

Why do I have to keep everything perfect?
  What am I trying to imitate?
    What am I trying to be?

My papers aren't allowed to have even the slightest crease...
  Maybe because I have so many creases...
    and crinkles... and tears...

I am a wrinkled page.
No matter how many times I try to smooth it against the table;
  the dents, the marks,
    the wears and tears of my life
      still remain.

But no matter the crinkle or tears...
    of a paper with value...
      a dollar, in this case...
It will still have a value of a dollar...

So I guess...
    no matter how many crinkles and tears this dollar has...
      My value is still great.

I guess I'll still be valued.
I guess I'll still be wanted.
I guess I'll be worth spending time...
      Yet... I still don't feel like it.

As Others Do

I dream,
as others do.
Though, mine
don't seem to come true
as others do.
But I'll keep dreaming anew
and do nothing to few
about these dreams,
as others do.

Wasting Time

Average life span in America is 78.64 years... 78.
365 days in a year.
24 hours in a day.
        8 hours for sleep.
        8 hours for work.
8 hours in a day.
7 days in a week.
        5 days of work.
72 hours in a week.

2 hours of eating a day...
So many TV shows...
I have friends...
I want to be friends with my friends...
        40 hours in a week...
I shower...
I brush my teeth...
I do chores...
and other things... like Facebook.
It's important to me...
        and everyone else.
I'll sleep in the days I don't work... I could use the sleep.
        Sleep is good for me.
14 hours in a week...
2 hours of freedom a day.
730 hours in a year of freedom.
That's...well...
56,940 hours in my lifetime... the average lifetime...
That's plenty... maybe. It is 2372.5 days...
        That's six years of freedom... almost seven.
Seven years to strive to be the best I can be...
to do what I want with my life;
have the career I want... 2 hours a day...
                but what if I sleep in longer?
What if I hang out with friends just a tad bit longer?
                  They're important to me.

But my career is important, too. I mean...
  it won't hurt to hang out with my friends
                a little longer.
But now I'm sad... I didn't expect this.
          I can't do anything when I'm sad.
Those two hours of freedom, are now two hours of worry,
                of self-doubt.

How can I work while hating myself?
How can strive when the one thing that is stopping me...
        Is me..?
I have such little time... will I waste it?
              Will I waste those two hours a day?

Sense > Cents

Twelve pennies is all I got.
I know it's not a lot.
However, it's all I brought.
At least I have more sense
than what others got.

Recess

Jimmy and Jen are swinging on the swings.

Kyle and Katie using strings to make things.

Daniel and Pierce are fighting a dragon to protect Clyde.

And a group of kids are taking turns on the slide.

Even though it's weird, Justin and Josh are watching each other pee.

But I'm just sitting on this bench, by myself...

Why won't anyone play with me?

I Can Not Save You

I am not a liberator of your addictions.
I am not a preserver of your contentment.
I am not a protector of your feelings.
I am not your savior.
I will not bring you salvation.
I am not your hero.
I carry no sword or shield.
I am not your guardian angel.
I do not carry that burden.

I cannot save you.
He who hath ears to hear, let him.
I do not carry the weight of steel,
but I do have ears.
I am a listener.
I can hear.
And if you speak,
I will listen.
I am an orator,
if that is what you want me to be.
I will speak.
If you listen,
you may be saved.
If you heed,
you may be liberated.
Although, only if you accept it.
If you perceive it,
then maybe you shall be saved.
But, I am no savior.
I can listen;
I can speak;
from either what I hear
or what I view.
But I am not your savior;
the saving has to be done by you.

Glass Tale

The feel of lava trickles on my wrists.
The wounds pulse to their own beat.
The lids to my eyes cannot mask the pain
as blood dances, when blade and skin meet.

The sun sets and drains into the bathroom sink.
The water brings back the clear skies
as I pat dad's new towel on my mistakes.
My curiosity reins my life.

My breath stops and my hopes take over.
The cloth is removed, as are my hopes.
I was still bleeding.
IT was still bleeding.

Control was lost, the whip was broken.
The lion continued to shout *Death*.
I step back as I lower my hand.
The mirror reflects my tale,
reflects my mistakes,
and is showing my future.

My sight weakens. Night is near.
"I won't do it again! PLEASE, let me last!"
The glass wipes me away from its face.
The chance... has passed.

Don't Touch My Butt

My butt is sensitive...

I know it's a cutie...
and maybe a bit perky...
But I let no one touch this booty!
It's just bizarre and quirky!

When someone grabs it,
I flinch!
Whether a grasp, a touch, or a pinch!
I halt and I don't move an inch!
And I won't relax or finally slump
until their hand backs away from my rump!

I don't let anyone touch my butt...
I don't care if I'm happy-
or if I'm in a rut!
Whether you're a king or queen
it's just obscene
to put your hand on my butt!

This might sound stupid
It might sound silly...
But I'd rather have you
straight-up grab my willie!

It doesn't bring me comfort!
It doesn't bring me pleasure!
It doesn't bring me happiness,
or any peace, when one
touches my treasure!

Well...
I straight-up sound like a nut.
There is one exception, though;
I do like it when you touch my butt.

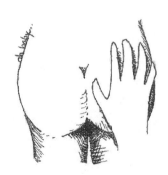

#Hashtag

#thIsworld
#haschanged
#fortheworse
#icant
#dealwithit
#nomore
#toomuch
#hashtags

#nolonger
#talking
#face2face
#slowlyslimming
#down
#ourconnections
#with @oneanother
#&verysoon
#wewill
#benothing
#with @eachother
#so
#pleasestop
#Imsotired
#icant
#handleit
#nomore

Life

What is life?
Is it a tangible clock that ticks away your existence?
Is it the physical impression of your evident status?
Or is it the mentality of how you feel?
Though erratic, according to certain questions and time periods in
life, it is all of these.

Life is a tangible clock that ticks away your existence.
It is undisclosed and anonymous, relying on what you have
consumed, or enclosed yourself in.
It changes on addictions, diseases, or calamities.
Altered by every action taken in the world, life becomes time,
or rather, death.

Life is the physical impression of your evident status.
It is reputation, it is substance, it is obvious.
Life is a mathematical equation, an accumulation of manifested
materials; what you corporally possess:
                    family, friends, objects, assets, and liabilities.
Life can be excellent or dreadful merely because you have no debt,
or a place to dwell;
regardless of feeling or its ticking clock.
Life is its own branch impervious to its other categories.

Life is the mentality of how you feel.
It is personality, it is sensitivity, it is action and reaction.
It is impervious, however, also influenced, or encouraged, by other
branches of life.
Nevertheless, it is independent, and free to alter the condition of
what life is within seconds.
Life is powered by emotion, not by reason.

So when people ask, "How is life?"
I guess it really just depends...

My Instrument

My fingers caress the keys so elegantly.
A roar of deep, hallow harmony.
Grease and sweat cause my hands to dance across this instrument,
burrowing each print into the notes which scream most of
desperation.
Clash of elemental sensations: Pain, Pleasure, Hate, and Love.
The stroke's reverberations kiss your eardrums and grant peace of
the heart.
The tempo of the keys ignites with a stronger bite, creating a sight
of light.
Colors and emotion! Lines brought to existence... with motion.
Graceful lines soaring and roaring to the impact of the tune.

Silence. However... a melody of peace.

The climax has been reached...
The Colors, the Emotion, the Lines, Keys, Sweat –
They all begin to preach!
Loudly they shout! With the greatest cry of desire!

To you, it's writing... to you... it's a tool.
A tool of society,
a device of ignorance,
a weapon of hate;
a keyboard.

To me – a piano... it is my instrument;
to write my words,
to listen to the music they create.
It is the lung for my emotions.

So let's play some music.

Poems These Days

So many poems are about love...
About all the people around who aren't "you"
        or the "you" you should be
                or could be...
I mean...
I understand... Love is a very strong
            and passionate
            and vague emotion.
With that, comes fear of being alone...
          That's a pretty big emotion.
But there are other emotions just as strong...
          and passionate
          and vague,
                 ...besides love.
Like...
The extreme hate I have toward asparagus.

Six Word Story

I can't
count.

Cigarettes and Coffee

I'm a workaholic.
I work all the time!
I have to keeping working
if I want to ever make a dime.

However, eventually I run
out of energy, awfully.
So I rely on other sources;
cigarettes and coffee.

I don't like drinking coffee,
but I have to.
So I fill it with creamer and sugar,
so I can take it down.
And it's so much sugar
it no longer stays brown!
It's extremely sweet,
one would think.
I still don't like it
it's just easier to drink.

I don't like smoking cigs,
but I have to.
I get menthol,
so I don't wreak.
It's easier to smoke, too.
Though, it makes Crest look weak.
But regular cigarettes are way too harsh,
and sometimes make me croak.
Even with menthol, I still don't like it;
It's just easier to smoke.

There are a few bad things
to cigarettes and coffee;
like, after all that energy,
I have to rest and recoup.

That's not the only thing though...
It makes me poop.

I don't like pooping,
but I have to.
Sometimes I put on cartoons,
or some good tunes
to make it more of an art
when I poop and fart.
So, I don't like 'em,
cigarettes or coffee...
I'm thinking of quitting.
Because out of all those things,
I'm really tired of shitting.

Pride

He was a man with big dreams, a big heart, yet not enough luck.
He didn't get the opportunities he deserved...
If he had... he would have run with them.
People cared about him... but not enough, I guess.

'Liking' a status, commenting, poking... 'saying' you're friends...
        That's not enough...
All he wanted... was people to be there.
All he wanted was for people to care.

                But he couldn't get that...

Sitting alone in the middle of the park... at 4am...
        And the cops didn't even ask... or show a bit of fucking
concern of why he was there!

He was a nobody...
        ...and shouldn't have been.
He was supposed to be somebody...
        He was supposed to be someone.
But no... all he got was a rotten life, a worthless job serving food...
        and possessions to imitate a better life.
He had no recognition from anyone.
His family didn't give two shits about him...
        why would anyone else?
Is it really hard to believe that he couldn't accept, or understand
                why anyone would love him?
And because no one understood that he feels the need to be fought
for...
        he pushed himself away from anyone that showed the
slightest attention...

It's not hard to break a leash made of string...
                even if interlaced with a thread of tender copper.

All he wanted...

      was to be truly loved...

      and to finally have an opportunity... just a chance.

         That's all he wanted...

And now he's gone; gone from our lives!

      He took the opportunity from all of you, this time.

He took the opportunity to love him, care for him, because you didn't take it.

            And so, I will be taking his place.

            The best part – you won't like me.

            I am not here to make friends.

            I am not here to be loved.

            I am here to fuck shit up.

            I am here to get a reason –

                  Steal a reason.

         A reason to keep this body breathing...!

              To try and give Him a legacy.

            I don't need luck.

I don't have a heavy past to weigh me down.

I don't have feelings.

I don't have a choice.

I was born to be this way.

      I was *created* to be this way.

I'm motherfuckin' **Pride**.

And it's nice to meet you...

      But I don't give a fuck about you...

         What matters...

            Is Me.

Touch Me

Touch me

Yes, just like that...

Hit me, I don't care...

Hit me harder, if you must...

Hug me...

Tight...

Or pat my back, I don't care...

Strangle me... Yell at me!

Grab me!

Throw me! I don't care...

Kiss me... bite my lip....

Show your hate!

I don't care...!

... as long as you touch me.

"I have seen the devil"

I see him in the morning...
I see him at night...
I see him wherever I drive...
I can't escape him...
I have tried. When
I have doubts or when
I am afraid...
I am never far enough from him...
I await his appearance when
I look into a store's entrance...
I can feel him upon the dock of the sea.
I have seen the devil...
I see the devil.
I see him in every reflection.
He stands where I stand.
He follows every step I take.
I have seen the devil...
I have seen...
I have...
I...
He sees me...
He has seen me...
He and
I are
Me.

Your Valentine

A day which should celebrate
a man who died;
who strived to revive
forgotten and banished men...

Instead, with little, to no thought
of the letter that was given
in a prison to woman only forgiven
by him;

We sweep away the origination
of the day, and replace it with carnations,
flowers, chocolates, and other hollow donations.

Spontaneous love;
roses of red in a large bouquets.
A battle unworthy of fighting...
Just to be with someone specifically on this day.

We all feel alone
when others' love is flaunted.
So, when a whole world is loving...
We feel even more unwanted...

So we must try our hardest
to do one of two things:
either sit and be alone...
or as someone accepts, we cling.

We become the kings and queens of clinging
until that fateful day arrives...
So, on that day, we may not have rings,
but we flaunt as if husbands and wives...

When, in reality, it's simply just another day...
Another day of dealing with sadness...
Or a day, like no other,
to just show your feelings for another.

This should be done every day of the year...
Loving the one you're with, always trying your best
to show how you truly feel, trying not to oppress
those feelings, waiting for a single day to confess
why you have invested this time with them...

This goes for fathers, brothers, or mothers...
or for a significant other...
Even your friends you can smother
with love on any day of the year...

You are not alone.
Do not be persecuted or forbidden
by the ones who flaunt
their momentary love.

You are loved.
And always show love.
Valentinus always did – he always tried.
February 14 is only the day that he died.

Insinuation

Yes, some relationships 'didn't work out,'
but there are other reasons why I am single...
The real reason is: I just don't know how to mingle.
It's not like it used to be...
Loving moments...
and words so powerful, they became quotations.
No. Now, things are over my head...!
People confusing politeness with flirtation
or strange and mysterious insinuations...

It baffles my mind...
and would ruin my life,
if I truly cared...

I just wish someone
would send me a memo
so I could at least be prepared;
or at least understand
the subject at hand.

But I don't need a memo to realize
romance is no longer
"thee's" and "thou's" or "long agos"...
it's just "hey guhs!"
and excessive innuendos.

And once,
I walked the streets engulfed
by the madness this new flirting supplied...
Yet, hope was awoken as I strolled
passed a beautiful, innocent pair of blue eyes.

"Hello there"
I fearfully whispered...
Her voice was alike the feeling
if I had kissed her.
It was a beautiful moment;
with a wonderful conversation...
And when the second came...
I counted to three,
but before I could speak, speak did she...

"Would you like to come have coffee with me?"
I nodded excitedly and asked her when and where;
and she provided directions on how to get there...

And that night
I approached her door around 7:30,
brushing off my shirt,
trying to not look too dirty.
And there I stood, with a coffee mug in hand,
and that door swung open...

I almost lost all control...
I felt like the biggest schmuck...
There she was standing in lingerie...
Apparently... down to fuck.

In the Fountain, My Doubtful Wish Goes

A coarse, bole, burnt, coin of copper and zinc...
And to think, of all the pockets it had been...
Now you meet it, at your feet.
A rugged, forgotten penny, disguised by concrete.
The weightless, forgotten hero meets your hand,
and the celestial fountain catches your eyes.
Your sanguine mind brings you to this pond of fish.
Conformed to culture, you prepare your wish.
Deep in thought, as symbolic as praying;
your hands create a swing, an elegant swaying.
Before this man leaves your hand, you already know
that it is just a formality. You doubt the throw.
You smirk with understanding of this lunacy.
You know that no matter how much you pray;
even with coins of plenty...
that your wish won't come true...
Because it's simply... a worthless, brown penny.

The Blind Man Sees

Born with darkness.
No color, no shapes... nothing at all.
Black is the only thing this man truly saw.

Years passed and the blindness never ended.
Failure flourished from all that was recommended.

"Maybe your eyes aren't what you should be observing.
Attention should be focused on areas more deserving."

The blind man sat guessing,
and things began linking.
It wasn't his eyes that were the problem;
it was his thinking.

Moments passed...
Vision – no longer a flaw.
After all the years of darkness...
the blind man finally saw.

Quiet Life

"Look at him, sitting alone at the party.
Hardly
giving a glance at anyone who walks by.
He must be really smart,
and quite intelligent guy!"
SAID NO ONE EVER!

Look at me, sitting alone at this party!
Hardly giving an eye at anyone who walks by.
But maybe if you try and see
what kind of person I would actually be,
you would know that I'm smarter and sharper
than anyone at this stupid party.

I can express my feelings.
I can cry and shout,
I can smile or frown.
I promise! But you doubt
me simply because you rather
compare me to these other people
who gather with beers in their hand,
talking about the bands
they can't stand.
Andif you would take the time to understand me;
or take the time to
Realize, that it's not because of you
or some higher power sham
that makes me this way –
it's who I am.

I know more than I say.
I think more than I can speak.
I see more than what you sheik,
pretentious animals could ever seek.

But I do not judge you
for being in this tree
of socialites who pretend to care;
pretend to be free!
And if I don't judge you,
what gives you the right to judge me?
I am fine with being alone.
I prefer to be it.
Even if you can't see it.

Maybe one day...
Maybe one day, I will give you permission
to see that it's not a condition;
it's not an affliction.
I am not fragile.
I am not anti-social.
I am not shy.
I am just a guy
you seem to stone.
I know who I am
and I have shown
that I CHOOSE this.
I choose to die alone.

People have tried to understand
and their minds have twirled;
confused as to why
I choose to live a quiet life
in this noisy, noisy world.

Resonance

Feed...
Burrow into recollection.
Augment what was.
What is.
What will.
What isn't.
What won't.

Twist the knife... Distort.
Amplify.

Kindle. Illustrate. Formulate.

Tremble. Throb... throb. pound.
Pulse... quiver... shiver. Sound.

Unity.
Opportunity.
Great!
Create.

Scribble. Scratch... Composition.
Remember. Revise. Repetition.

Execution.

Remorse...

...

of course.

Nothing Uncovered.
Nothing Discovered.
Nothing Recovered.

No benefit, no progress, nothing gained.
Just a man...
chained...
drained.
Here to explain
what I do during a very lonely night.

This is how I do it – how do you write?

To Whom It May Concern,

Something has come to my attention,
something that I've recently learned,
something I thought I should mention...
For it is knowledge that you have long yearned...

You will be worthless and hurt...
You won't even leave a stain in history.
You will be as crucial as a spec of dirt...
The cost for fearing Fate's mystery.

You will tremble for every second that passes
that you don't show an ounce of progression.
You will be intimidated by the success of masses
and eventually succumb to your own depression.

It will lead to blood –
Only your own.
It will lead to mud...
decorated by meaningless ink and stone.

Yet... before your last home is hollowed;
Fate will be reality, and you will write a letter.
A letter to your former self, followed
by hopes that he can do things better.

Yet, as worthless as your breath,
you will understand, at last.
It is pointless...
to try and change the past.

So what started as resistance against fate,
has merely become a declaration:
That it is only the future you can dictate...
And ignoring that... will lead you to my damnation.

In conclusion...
You know what's to come...
Regards.
And adieu.

                                    To Me,

                                    From,
                              Future You

Snowy Night

Where others prefer day,
I prefer night.
Where others prefer color,
I prefer white.

Where others pray
for sunlight and clear skies,
I welcome the darkness
and the blue, disguised
by clouds, unifying the hues
to a single monochromatic scheme,
infused with white, grays, and blacks.
I pray for a snow.
A blanket absent of tracks.

This is not silence of the winter,
this is stillness and tranquility.
Where others see weakening,
I see purity.

I see trees and bushes
in the simplest forms, excelling
alone with perfection.
And in each of these dwellings
during the winter...
are families, finally giving attention
that they have lacked for all these years
because of life's mundane interjections.

Where the white embers of winter
are hated by the majority,
I stand outside in harmony
and adore it's authority.

Where others prefer to stay inside,
away from the winter's bite,
I prefer to stay outside
and enjoy this seamless, snowy night.

It's Ok

My pencil broke!
But the ideas didn't stop!
But I realized it's mechanical...
So, I just pressed the eraser on top.

My World

In my world, everything makes sense.
In my world, it's all me!
I choose who lives.
I choose who dies.
I choose who smiles...
and who cries.

In my world, I am free.
I can be around who I want.
And I can be whatever I've wanted to be!

The grass is greener on either side.
The sky is always filled with rainbows,
and unicorns.
They are beautiful...
with long majestic horns!

I love my world.
I'm with the person I love...
And in my world, I'm not human...
Well... kind of.

In my world, it's never
too cold, or too hot.
It's just perfect.
It's my world! So, why not?

Why shouldn't it be perfect?!
This world is ideal!
In my world, I'm free...
And don't you dare try to steal
it away from me!

In my world...
I will never be sad.
I will never be mad.

Oh, I love my world so much.
Because when I'm not in my world...
The world you can't touch...
I am in your world,
filled with gloom.
Oh, how I hate
this pillowed, white room.

Lost In Mist

Has the spark been lost on the account of the rainy solitude my
cloudy vision fostered?
It is hard to see even the slightest ember in this mist.
Can faith brighten that flame?
Or is there no light left to brighten?
And how long shall I tread in my simulated haze
before I realize that the glimmer was merely false hope of an ever-
burning torch.

My Perfect Room

This my room…
It's perfect;
from ceiling to floor!
Everything is perfect.
The drawer,
my glass desk,
and my perfect door.

My file cabinet,
my closet,
and my shelf of movies and books
are perfectly organized.
It's aesthetically pure;
alphabetically, for sure!
Wouldn't have it any other way…
It's symmetrical and square
every moment of the day.
Anywhere you stand,
where ever you laid.
Everything is perfect.
My bed sheets – always made!

Ah yes…
My room is perfect.
From far away! Or close-up!
The only issue, I can't move…
because I don't want to mess it up.

Happy Birthday, Darling

The sound of the blinds awaken your eyes
to a light too bright, causing your lids to flee.
A smell comes near; someone is here!
Surprise! You open your eyes to me.

And on your chest I begin to rest
a small table of items and food.
A stack of French toast, also some juice,
and a rose just to set the mood.

I look into your eyes, smile and spring,
"Now, I have a few things to say-"
I start to pace, as if solving a crime,
"and please forgive me, if I begin to rhyme."

Swiftly I decide that I'm not going to stand.
Instead, I kneel; and grab a hold of your hand.
"You have been an astounding girl to me,
and to be a part of the celebration of your birth...
is a blessing to see."

"You are a beautiful creation, with a personality so unique...
And I can claim you...
I can claim... this elegant form of life...
Only one day is greater than this day... and it's a day I seek.
Only one day is greater than celebrating your life.
And that's the day that I can call you my wife."

Wrath

I am your silent rage.
I am your gaze of retribution.
My heart drums a militia rhythm.
My veins stomp in unison.
My lips form fire.

I am Wrath.
I do not allow my quaking chin to liberate my lips.
I do not allow my swollen hands to clench
for I know where my will lies.
Chains of the heaviest metal
could not hold my muscles from tensing,
but I can.
Through your windows, I am serene.
I do not allow you to see my fury.
I will grin, grating my teeth...
but you will see a smile.
I will cackle, with my skin still....
but you will hear a laugh.

You do not hear the crackling of the fuse...
but you will be there for the show.

I will be sudden.
I will be unanticipated...
I WILL be silent.
You WILL die by my hand.
And then, I shall allow you to see
Wrath.

Beer is Gross

It's an acquired taste they say;
Beer, that is.
With it's nasty, nastiness...
and it's fizz!
Its disgusting smells,
from lagers to lite.
It all disgusts me;
from any time...
day to night.
I tried a cider once,
"You'll like it, it's sweet!"
So I tried it...
The first sip was neat...
But when I took another...
I lost control.
I spit it out. In his face!
"You lying asshole!"
It was gross...
"If you drink it more...you'll like it.
Or maybe drink it quicker!"
So I did... and beer is gross...
Fuck it, I'll stick to liquor.

Firebreak
A man dressed in black
and eyes of golden brown.
A man that never smiled,
nor did he frown.

His only friends
was that of wood and steel;
and a journal
of all the feeling that he would feel.

However, by another,
when the hide of this diary turned,
the ink and binding would vanish
and each of the pages would burn.

The fire would continue to glow
and the history would stack.
A pile crafted of ashes;
all dressed in black.

Gl-ass

Today I found
glass in my shoe...
And it cut me!
My foot is red and blue...!

But I'm thankful it was only that...
Otherwise, I wouldn't have the cash
if it was anywhere serious...
like my ass.

Pertus Occulir

Lying on his palm, a silver necklace rested.
He, with it, questioned the money and time he invested.
A necklace... With a heart, a ribbon, and a unique kind of branding.
A necklace for someone exceptionally special... and outstanding.
But with a quick grasp, a realization occurred.
His whole vision was swiftly blurred.
The twinge and torture matured and persisted.
A necklace for a girl, that never existed.

So the necklace was placed in dark chest, on a bed of red.
And before the box was shut and locked, he said,
"Looks like I'll sit and wait, and be alone again...
But she would have loved it. Whoever it might have been."

New Year

There is one moment...
A single moment...
Where each mind –
Every person –
Every thought...
contains happiness.
Joy.
Hope.
Peace.

In this moment, people look up;
not only at the spark of lights that project colors
and illuminate everything beneath them.
Not only are they looking up at a figment of time...
an illusion of time resetting...
They are dreaming!
They are thinking of one thing.
Hope.

'In ten seconds, I can be different.
I can have another chance
at being what and who I want to be.'

Their thoughts are taken over by what is soon to come.

Hate.
Doubt.
Worry.
Absent.

Hope overwhelms their thoughts
and sets aside any negativity.

In this moment
everything is perfect.

It is a new year.
It is my time to shine!
This will be my year!

I adore this illusion...

For that last second... peace.

But for that first second...
To them, nothing has changed.
They expect immediate renewal.
In this new moment... every thought...
every person...
is desolate.

That first second...
Misery.

But there will always be next year.

San[in]ity

There are tears running through my bones.
I can feel them engulfing the joints in my fingers...
But... they're gone.

Not tearless... those are still running...
Boneless... Finger...less.

My elbows are still...
no...

The water... it should come out the eyes...
Right...?
My chin... tells me I am crying...
But I just feel my throat... swelling with the very-no...
Not my throat... my chest... yes... it tickles...
But I'm not giggling anymore...

I wish...

Please! Why is it so much easier to frown?
Why does smiling hurt...so...much....

They have nowhere to go anymore...
..I'm sorry... you have taken every path you could...
My body is...

it's gone...

Strong Habit

Respect:
a lost entity in this rusted cage.
Indescribable:
the pain I endure when others lack the simple ability to be honest.

I am annoyed at the boorish people that can't simply tell another...
...it's the end.

So, assume, or imagine, a world with no trust, no love.
Assume the one you adore is taking your love and affection and
burning it, inhaling it...
watching it burn,
and kissing another
with the rotten, leftover taste of the relationship you had.

But with that simple intake,
know that when that habit is strong enough, and inhaled enough;
a plague... a cancer...
will engulf their body.
And as they lie in that hospital bed, they will regret that habit.

Know that there is no cure, except one...
One cure:
waiting for that last inhale they took to kick in,
          ...and set a solid rhythm to the machine next to them.

The White Dot on the Black Page

Invisibility. A privilege or a curse?
I can vanish in the middle of a drunken crowd,
disappear when sitting next to light.
Yet, not just any light.
The light that doesn't realize how bright it shines.
Maybe I balance that light.
Next to me it shines brighter.
The contrast attracts these bugs of interest.
It is a white dot on a black page. I am its black page.
Though the darkness absorbs all of the space,
that white dot reveals everything the rest of the page has to offer.
So why not rid of the page and leave that little, white dot?
Because without it… no one knows what light is.

The One You Never Knew

I am somebody...
Maybe...
I care.
I feel.
I hide...
I feel all emotion.

I am weary.
I am done in by your effort to assume you comprehend me.

Continue your endeavor.
At least until you grasp the idea that you will finish with no success.
I am your scissor.
I am here, at this time, to shatter your reflection...
I want you to know:
I am who I am, and you cannot prevail... and you will not win.
Every flesh contains more flesh... the flesh within me is not real.
        So you say...
Every remark and each expression you craft with your flesh,
ruptures mine.
I will consent to, what you would call, illusory hemorrhaging,
as you pass on those slurs.
Though... I can only bleed for so long.
Once this instance... this engagement approaches...
When my death comes, you will surely see,
that the blood is real, and you never knew me.

One Tit, Two Tit
One tit,
two tits,
nice tits,
ew tits.

Black tits,
other tits,
old tits,
new tits.

Certain tits
have scars.

Look at ours!
Wow! What a lot
of tits there are.

Indeed. Some are nice. And some are ew.
Some are old. And some are new.
Some are sad.
And some are glad.
And some tits are very, very bad.

Why are they
sad and glad and bad?
I do not know.
Google it...
Don't ask your dad.

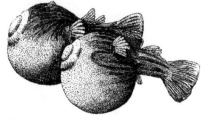

Some are thin.
And some are fat.
Some are clean
and some have tats.

From there to here,
From here to there,
Tits are thankfully
everywhere.

Some of these tits are perky
and some of them sag.
Some we don't talk about
and others we brag.

Some are let open
and some are oppressed.
But I tell you one thing, my friend.
My favorite type of tits,
Wanna take a guess?
Yes, tits on women,
are the tits I like the breast.

Vanity

A generation goes
and another comes;
yet, the earth remains forever.

The sun rises
the sun sets
and hastens... to rise again.

The wind travels north
the wind travels south
and it shall do so again.

All the rivers run into the sea
yet, the sea is not full.
To the place from which the rivers came
to there they shall return again.

The thing that has been
is to be again.
Which has been done
shall be done again.

There is nothing new
under this sun:
the sun that has always been.

You may be wise
and wield your eyes
in your mind.

You may be foolish
and walk blind
into darkness.

Yet, in the end,
whether the fool or wise...
there is no eternal remembrance...
In the days to come,
All shall be forgotten.
And so, how shall the wise man die?
Lost and forgotten,
just as the fool.

There is time to be born...
and a time to die.
A time to weep,
a time to laugh.
A time to get,
A time to lose.
A time to love,
A time to hate.
A time for war,
A time for peace.

It is all hollow...
It shall return eternally.
Death is the only outcome of man.
Thus, pleasure the breath you bear.
Bestow that pleasure on others.

For a good name is better than precious perfume.
And the day of death is better than that of birth.
Finer it is to visit a house of mourning than a house of feast.
As that is the end of all men; and the living shall lay it to heart.
Better is the end of a thing than the beginning.

Nevertheless, it is all vanity.
We shall all go to one place.
All are of the dust
and all shall turn to dust again.

Logic

I was given a gift... since birth, I've had it.
A unpleasant talent... forced down my throat:
to look at the world as the granter desired:

"A world of creatures left uninspired.
Creatures of hate, of greed, and absolute power –
Mortals that let emotions devour
their thought – their needs – their biological functions.
Instead of treating their recycled dysfunctions."

They – These 'people' were awarded the ability to think... and
adoration.
Yet they celebrate abuse and fornication.
There are some, whom are driven positively by emotion,
but are hindered by challenges because their devotion.

However, the observation of society's lack of varieties
was not the gift that I was given... I was given nothing.
No emotion...no lust... and it feels like treason.
Left with nothing... except the gift of reason.
It may seem ok – but... it's perverted...
Because of my gift, I feel deserted.

It Was Me

I hear you shouting and crying.
I hear you bellow every name you know;
hoping that someone will come and help.
But no one will come.
They are scared.
We are scared.
We are guilty.
That's why we are not coming to aid you.

I, especially, cannot help you...
Because I have the most guilt.
I have the most fear.

So shriek as loud as you can...
Scream from the soul.
I really am sorry...
I didn't replace the toilet paper roll.

Wayward Forest

I am bewildered by this beauty...
You should be, too.
No land is as exquisite as this timeless forest.
Look! The trees! They're mingling and melding with the sunlight.
Oh! But the bark is just as marvelous!
Look at that craftsmanship; how masterly Mother Nature's hand is.
So detailed. So defined. Telling ancient, untold stories...
"Get out" is what it reads...
However, I am too dazed by its intricacy to read the warnings...

Around us, beneath the bark and light...
Diversity... fruits of plenty!
The water is dripping so slowly on the fruits... caressing them,
as a loving man caresses his wife.
A soft... gentle touch...

How tantalizing.
I can only dream of what they would taste.
So luscious... and ample... certain to be cursed by God.

This forest carries plenty, yet only bears the harmonious sound of
rustling leaves...
Not just rustling... but... whistling.
Watch! They pucker their lips and whistle...
They are whistling to us!
Or... speaking to us...
"Get out..." is what they mouth.
However, my eyes are closed, and I am too soothed by this
symphony to listen.

This forest sings...
Do you hear its song?
This forest possesses so many splendors...
Yet, only the sound of wind...
Do you hear any birds chirping along the forest's song?
I don't...

Not even a rabbit rustling in the bushes...
Wait...
Did you hear that?
Behind you... a rustling in that berry bush!
It's shaking to the song of the forest! Like maracas!
"Get out..."

How heavenly...

Wait... that's not a rustle... it's... It's a rattle.
... I remember now. We've been here before...
I was so distracted by all this beauty... that...
I forgot why I left before... I knew this pain would come. But...

Those fangs fit so nicely into the pores of my skin...
as perfect as how tender hands hold.
I feel its venom... intertwining with my blood...
Just as lips merge so seamlessly with another...

I came back for this...
All of this beauty... and I came back for the bite.

I am bewildered by this beauty...

Wow, Really?

By the fiend's neck I gripped the sword tight,
the destruction of life is what happened tonight.
The power of ice left the breathing still...
The fire that burned from the Warlock's thrill...
And I, a knight of all that is holy
is rotting away... and dying slowly.
My grades consumed...
My addiction resumed...
It absorbed my pain...
But drove me insane...
I gave up on life... for a game.

I realize where this knight of light is now...
it's me, living inside of WoW.

Safe

Cars drive fast
Cars drive slight
And lives go fast
When running the light!

An Apple a Day

'An apple a day, keeps the doctor away.'
But I didn't eat an apple today,
Nor did I eat an apple yesterday.

"You can't be serious!
My intake of fruit affects other people?"
The saying is as real as they say...
After these past two days... it's hard to ignore
these two doctors, standing at my front door,
gazing up at the floor I live.

"It cannot be."
I said with fright.
"Eat your apples and we'll leave!"
They shouted, in their coats of white.

"No. No more apples!
I can't stand to eat another bite!
So get off my lawn!
Good night!"

And so I slept to the sound
of two doctors whispering
about their apples,
but I was not listening.

About a week later,
I looked out my door.
And by my surprise...
the doctors grew by four!

"What the hell?!
What are you here to achieve?!"

"If you eat your apples...
Then we'll leave.
Until that moment
I'm afraid we can't."

All of this from a stupid plant...

A tree or whatever...
I decided to go back to sleep,
until I thought of something clever.

However, I was awoken
in the middle of the night...
By six or more doctors
in lab coats of white.
I was tied down to my bed
by each of my limbs.
They pulled out a bag of apples,
and sung a sort of hymn.
In unison... what a sight.

"Tonight you will eat your apples.
We tried to keep our space.
But you ignore us."
And so they stuffed my face.

At first I was disgusted...
Then I couldn't breathe...
So many apples...

They would drive these apples into my mouth.
I had about five down my throat.
I've never experienced so much dread...
All because I found apples disgusting...
Good thing you can't taste things when you're dead.

Damnation

This feeling...
feelings..
...awe and fright.

The need to hold, the need to kiss...
Two things that I miss.
Fear of what you may convey
is what pushes me away.

Fixation, Temptation, Elation, Damnation.

From flirtation came my admiration and determination...
the foundation to conversation.
This foundation led to the realization vaccination,
lack of realization would prevent frustration and damnation.
So I thought.....

Fading vaccination... probation... confirmation... damnation...
...all began with education...
realization that education taught me how to read...
how to read what you said.

The test is over, most would agree.
however I'm blind, you see.
Not because of circumstances of the stricken
but reason of force.

I sit there with a pencil in hand,
and a clock that's ticking,
but no test at the desk.

The test isn't over...it can't be over.
For others it would be...
..but...the test isn't over...
 not for me...

The "Blind" Side

Sometimes I feel blessed I live in a blind world.
I haven't decided whether it helps me, or destroys me.
Maybe it's good.
Judgment is irrelevant...
I can't see your beautiful face, the tattoo on your right arm, or the messenger bag you carry everywhere you walk.
I have to trust you.
I have to believe your personality will create your presence.
I have to believe your words will forge your wardrobe.
But... the good thing may very well be equally as bad.
I can't enjoy your smile that illuminates the world.
I can't see the hidden lies behind those hazel facades.
I will never truly be able to embrace the composer of those musical words.
I just have to trust your personality can form it for me.

Chyea right...

Charles, the Wise
and Paul, the Lazier of the Eyes

"Hello there, human.
My name is Charles, the wise.
And this my brother, Paul.
The lazier of us eyes.

I hope our appearance
doesn't frighten you, too greatly.
But we thought we would introduce ourselves,
because we've been pretty bored lately.

I mean...
I know we're eyeballs
directly from the socket..
But we're the size of a...-
a... Well, Your socket!
And we could fit easily in your pocket!

So, I beg you, kind human.
We are nice eyes, so don't retreat.
I mean... Who would be scared
of eyeballs in a top hat and sheet?

I guess the thought...
That we're eyeballs... and we speak..
I guess that could
make about anyone shriek.

To explain; I am telepathic...
Paul doesn't really talk. Although,
it may be just because the writer said so?

Darn! Distracted!

Anyways, it what a pleasure
in meeting someone as quiet as you.
Although, you not talking may be
what the writer wanted you to do."

My Wall

It isn't too bad behind this wall...
It's built up very, very tall.

I don't get an ounce of light, at all!
It isn't too bad behind this wall...

No one can get to me at all.

(To Be Continued)

Goodbye Rose

This rose hasn't wilted...
Your petals still bloom in splendor.
Your scent... still alluring...
This rose... beautiful, forever.

This rose has not lost a petal...
nor has it lost its grace...

The disgrace of it all...-
The shame I bear...
The despair of knowing...
Merely after a minute...
Doubt and worry... Is what I began sowing...

And more minutes passed...
Days kept going...
Months, we lasted.
Doubt still growing...

And soon to rise from dirt,
constructed of anxiety and pain,
arose fear, barbs, and vigorous chains...

Chains...
That I have made...
To lock me down...
To push you away...
To keep me still
So you can stay...
Beautiful...

I shall blossom regret...
and you shall sway to another breeze...

Do be at ease...
These new thorns suit me well.

I know it's hard to understand
Or see...
I just want you to be beautiful...
So, I saved you from me.

Jimmy

This is Jimmy!

Jimmy got a new phone!

It's all white –
with a cool ring tone!
He's got all sorts of apps
and all sorts of games...

He has Chirpy, Headbook, the Sight of Names!
He has Vegi-Ninja and Happy Birds!
He has them all... even Wacky Birds!

But while Jimmy was on a game fishing...
what all, outside the phone, was he missing?

He had tons of friends he talked to, on his phone.
But when it went black... he was all alone.

How long did Jimmy spend looking down?
How much happened around?
Now, with his new white phone... powered down and black,
Little Jimmy is sad...
because all that time he wasted.
Now, Jimmy can't get that back.

No More Long Days and Nights

Up in Alaska,
where the air is freeing.
There was a being,
watching everyone skiing.
He had pearlescent black eyes,
and thin, pointy nose.
His name was Nix,
he wore a long black scarf
and all white clothes.
He doesn't remember
how he appeared;
but he knew that to all
the children, he was revered.
For years he played
with all these toddlers.
He felt appreciated
and respected; like a father.
But after a decade or two,
he got tired of all these snowball fights
and hide and seek,
during these long days and long nights.
And although the children
would definitely disprove,
he decided to pack up
and move.
To Florida, he would go.
Where all the old people strolled!
And on the plane he went,
thankful that the AC kept it cold.
And as he got off the plane
he smiles as big as he can.
But then he died...
Because Nix was a snowman.

These Are the Feelings I Feel

I do not have words worthy of comparison
to even the most mediocre of poets.
If I could express it like the artists express it...
maybe I could show it.
If I could write how the writers write...
then maybe I could confess it.
And maybe one day I may possess it,
or maybe upon a 'dreary night,'
possess that power that is required for writers
to write how writers write.
It is sad to say... I cannot reveal that gift,
even though I may feel those feelings, I cannot sift
through words or shift them around to form the perfect depiction
of the bluest skies, the greenest grass, or the flawless loving fiction.

The writers speak with such finesse,
"Let us gaze into the stars and caress
each other under moonlight and stars.
Away from buildings! Away from cars!
Let our love flourish and it shall last forever.
In my heart, I believe in our love, without a doubt."

I may feel those feelings, but I still say,
"Wanna hang out?"

The writer says, "How art thou, beautiful angel?"
The girls go wooing...
But no girl listens to:
"How you doing?"

"Lost are the words to describe the sorrow
and pain that I undergo in this rejection"

"Rejected because I lack the collection
of words to say how I feel."

"Bestowed this treacherous curse of being
a straw in a bundle of hay. The end draws nigh!"

"It sucks being just a normal guy..."

And it is very sad to say that, by God,
I am constricted to just simply cry.
I do not have a beautiful description,
for I am cursed as a normal guy.
A normal guy with normal feelings.
And sadly, these feelings cannot be written
or spoken in any outstanding way.
If I am sad, then I am just sad,
because that is all a normal guy can say.

OTHER STUFF

JUST REAL QUICK-ISH...

I am

During my eleventh grade year, I walked into my Physics class with the intention to continue my expertly crafted habit of falling asleep. I had developed the classic technique of placing my head on my arm and using my long hair as a curtain to conceal my real agenda. I walked to my desk as if the day was unlike any other. Little did I know, today was going to be different.

As I surveyed the classroom, I noticed that Ms. Phillips was not in sight. In her usual spot, sat a slim, African-American man in an all-black suit. I rested in my chair and laid my books on the floor. As my head rose, the door to the classroom shut. The man in the suit was standing in front of the door with his hand still caressing the knob.

He posed a question to an unsuspecting class, "How do you know purple is purple?"

There was silence as the students sat with a dumbfounded composure, as if they had all entered a coma of deep introspection. None of my classmates knew what the man in the suit was asking, so, naturally, they didn't attempt to respond. Following the initial silence, there was a loud silence. It was deafening.

Then I felt it; the sudden urge to humour the classroom's new-fangled, rocket scientist. No longer bound by hesitation, I shouted from the back of the classroom with a smirk, "The color purple is the color purple because all of the other colors it is not."

The man in the suit halted in astonishment. Checkmate.

My smirk quickly ceased as the man in the suit smiled, as if there was a chess piece I didn't see. "Now... How does this relate to you?"

For once, I was aphonic. Oblivious.

"Just like the color, you are who you are because of what you're not, or what you don't want to be." He continued grinning as he patrolled around the classroom, further refining his allusion. "Your history makes you who you are. Of course, without the people incorporated in your past, the people you loved, hated, or even ephemeral acquaintances; how could you have a history? Who would you be? With the absence of who you aren't, you can not be."

His influential words echoed. His voice became my own. "I am what I'm not. Without what I'm not, I can't be."
From that moment on, it rang just like the bells of a church on Sunday morning. It burrowed, and flourished into my heart. I began cherishing the people around me and recognizing the effect they have on me. Despite the rejuvenating contentment of this radical gratitude, it wasn't soon after that I had realized the tribulation. My father.

My reflection to the past, the instances with my father, shattered my enchantment. I recall his selfishness, his financial vices, his habitual smoking and drinking, and specifically, his exclusion of blood. That is what led me to my collapse. That's what got me here. I feasted from depression, I reached my pinnacle, and this is what was harvested. Everything he was and everything he did; iniquity.

Yet, I am not bitter or saddened. I am content. Seeing, if he wasn't there. Who would I be? If he weren't there, who would I be? Would I be?

Without my father, without my strife, without my triumphs - I cannot be. Without the divorce, without family, without heartache, without solitude, and without my reliable perception – I cannot be. In the absence of these things, I cannot be. Be that as it may, these things are present. These things are real.

I am.

Fading With Formality

When given the moment to think... I think too much.
I've been thinking about every person that sits on my little "friend's list."
And I watch them fade... fade slowly away from friendship and develop into a formality.

I think about everyone, and I wish I could have a conversation with each of them –
tell them how I feel and how much I miss them.
Maybe it's because of the solitude that I reside in that makes me feel so strongly about these people;
these people I don't know, barely know, or have seen once.
But these people are family to me. I would give anything to those I have only shred a second for, or for those I even built up hate for.

It may be attention I seek, it may be love I hunt, or maybe to fill the love I simply lacked.
Whatever it may be, it has created a love I cannot explain.
These people are my brothers and sisters.
However, this formality.. has torn – not torn, slower...
It has shredded the family I did have and forced them into abandonment; a prison of protocol.
I came blame the formality, though. It's just a habit.
A habit that I probably created. Manipulated, scarring myself at every glance.
A list of all those I've done wrong, of all those I've done right.
A check list of my morality.

I wish I could return. Back to what I had before this list.
But the formality is set. To most... this is a procedure to forget.
I have not forgotten.
I may fade into these customs and rituals.
I may seem like I have forgotten.
However, as long as this list stands strong.
I will never forget what I've done right...
or who've I've done wrong.

Anguish ~~Wanted~~ Needed

These tungsten skulls cannot be pierced by the will of it's beholder,
Nor can the bearer's mind be altered or cured by the words of the
wise.
They cannot change simply because they want to... or because it's
the best thing to do.
That takes effort, that takes the strongest will, and these protesters
rather the simplicity of routine.
Because it's easy.
It's easier to be sad...
It's easier to blame someone else, rather than ourselves.

If you take the sun away from our universe, the one thing that
provides light, and we reside in darkness – it's our natural
surroundings.
Our minds mirror that structure. It takes determination and strength
to enforce light on something that is naturally dark.
So we reside in it, we let it determine our fate, our destiny; it
becomes our soul.
Because it's easy.

Even a torch lit in a cavern seems hopeless, for we still cannot see.
We leave the cavern the way it is, because lighting one torch was,
what we feel, the hardest thing in the world.
We let our caves reside in darkness, even if all it takes is another
torch to see.
Why would we go get more torches, or more flint and tinder just to
light up a cave?
And so, dark, it shall remain to be.

What could this cave hold?
Bumps, and holes, bats, or mold.
It could hold all of pain and displeasure.
There could be nothing. But there could be treasure.
Without enough effort... without enough light,
you will trip, you will fall, you may die.

You will never discover an ounce of yourself, and only experience pain.
Worst of all, if you do not try, unknown is what your cave will remain.

Sadly, the only thing that seems to push these people is... absolute anguish.
An occurrence constructed of lightning, to pierce even the strongest plated skull.
One that whispers the sounds of sirens and nuclear warfare.
Only with pure chaos does one seem to be granted with aspiration.
However, like lightning, it is random and everyone cannot be stricken.
It is truly sad... that this is what it takes.
It takes one extreme, sad occurrence to push people to motivated or happy.

I hope people understand; I am not trying to represent a sadistic, inhuman being.
I just want people to try harder. I want people... just to be happy.
And I really don't want lightning, but it seems to be the only way...
So, if I have to be the evil one, I will take that form.
I wished for everything else, and it didn't work, so now I pray for storms.

Lamp

I can't say sorry anymore. I'm not sorry for every thought and word I don't hold back. I've tried so hard to be that simple machine that catches an occasional eye; an inanimate object that takes a moment out of your life. As you grasp and admire my hand carved, wooden designs, I lighten the room gently enough to still call it darkness.

I flicker at your sudden motion, your transition from wood to cloth. The neatly folded covering that holds in everything that is too strong for your eyes.

I try so hard to be that entity, but I am doomed.
As your cheeks and lips form a thankful smile, I flicker twice more.

On.

Off.

On.

Off.
Your smile fades and the wires within spark and jump. Dead. If only you could see what you couldn't see. Everything. The volts reflected every bit of glass and plastic. Contained enough to explode.
But no matter... I will be replaced. For I am just a lamp...

an inanimate object that catches an occasional eye. That is all.....I am.

WELL...
THAT'S THE END

ONE MORE...

Poetry

I love poetry, more than any other art.
Language has form and grammar.
Design as guidelines and rules.
Art has its audience, even if fools,
they determine what's good or bad.
Even though, they have no right to
determine what art is, but they do.

But poetry can be bent...
Poetry is a painting of emotions
spilled onto a single, white piece of paper.
Our minds forged by black ink.
It can be direct or abstract.
It can inward or outward.
It can be taken literally or figuratively.
It can be taken...
But only the writer knows that black ink
as a blind man reads a book.
The writer feels it with his mind; with his hand.
And no one can judge this man.
Because there is no rules to feelings.
There is no rules to poetry.

He doesn't have to be author.
He doesn't need talent or skill.
Just an ability to write and feel.
And he shall be a poet
and no one can disagree.
No has the right to.
Because it's poetry.
So do not attack.
Let the writers write in peace.
Let them paint in black.

DEDICATION

I dedicate this book to many –
from family to friends, or anyone to take a look...
or even the ones who dare to spend a penny
or more on this horrid and dreadful book.

I dedicate this feat to the 'famed' –
the few, at least... that inspired me greatly...
But I thank especially – those I'll name –
my best friends... Daniel, Pierce, and Katie!

I could honestly write a list...
It would probably go on and on...
and many would be pissed...

But the true person I must thank...
the one that introduced me to my calling...
Is none other than my good friend Molly.

She taught me to speak!
Write my feelings! Show my fright!
Show my pain – create my own technique!
She taught me how to write...

Without her...
I'd be wordless.
worthless...
So... Thank you, Molly...
and to all of those who impacted me mostly.
Without you, I could never write bad poetry.

Made in the USA
Lexington, KY
22 February 2017